PIANO ALL THE WAY

(Level Two)

T0080163

Foreword

Level Two of **PIANO ALL THE WAY** introduces the following concepts in

THEORY:

1. Bar lines and measures.
2. Note recognition in relation to the keyboard, and key association in relation to notation. A reading range of

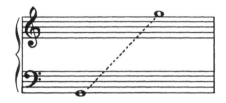

is covered.

3. Quarter time signatures: $\frac{2}{4}$ $\frac{3}{4}$ $\frac{4}{4}$ $\frac{6}{4}$
4. Major and minor chord patterns on the keyboard and the printed page.
5. Transposition.
6. Sharp, flat and natural signs.
7. Counting note and rest values in relation to pulse.
8. Thirteen major scales and their Tonic and Dominant Seventh chords.
9. Repeat signs; 1st and 2nd endings; Da Capo; Fine.
10. Interval recognition from Major 2nds through octaves.
11. Eighth note rhythmic patterns in quarter time.
12. Tie and octave signs.

TECHNIC:

1. Staccato, accent and portato touches.
2. Non-legato and legato pedaling.
3. Fluency in scale passages and broken chord arpeggii.

INTERPRETATION:

1. Tempo and mood indications.
2. Dynamics and shading signs.
3. The fermata.

EAR TRAINING:

1. Drill in recognizing major and minor triads.
2. Pitch location on the keyboard.

W. M. Co. 9585

Unit 1
NOTE RECOGNITION

Notes printed on the lines and spaces of the Treble Staff and the Bass Staff show which keys to play.

Notes from Middle C upward are printed on the lines and spaces of the

TREBLE STAFF

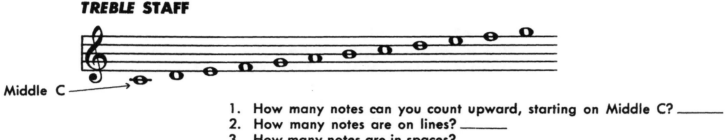

Middle C

1. How many notes can you count upward, starting on Middle C? _____
2. How many notes are on lines? _____
3. How many notes are in spaces? _____
4. As your teacher points, starting on Middle C and moving upward one note at a time, play each note and say if it is a Line or a Space.

Notes from Middle C downward are printed on the lines and spaces of the

BASS STAFF

Middle C

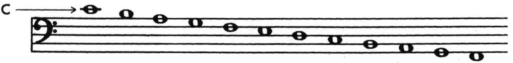

1. How many notes can you count downward, starting on Middle C? _____
2. How many notes are on lines? _____
3. How many notes are in spaces? _____
4. As your teacher points, starting on Middle C and moving downward one note at a time, play each note and say if it is a Line or a Space.

The **TREBLE STAFF** and the **BASS STAFF** combined make the

GRAND STAFF

The R. H. usually plays all the notes on the 𝄞

R. H. Middle C

L. H. Middle C

The L. H. usually plays all the notes on the 𝄢

Brace

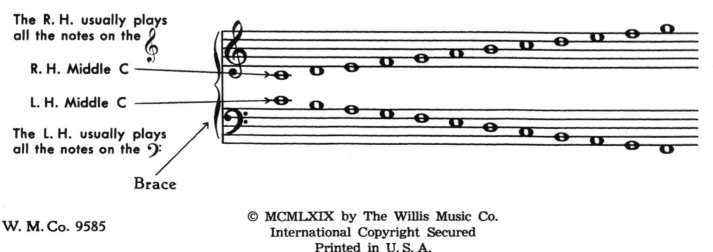

W. M. Co. 9585

FINDING NOTES UP AND DOWN FROM MIDDLE C

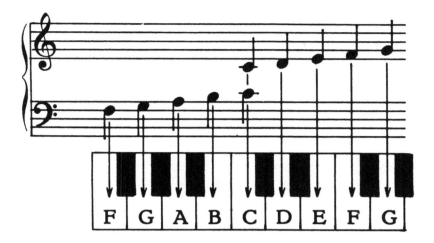

Name and play the notes in the following exercises: (Use any fingers.)

1. Example

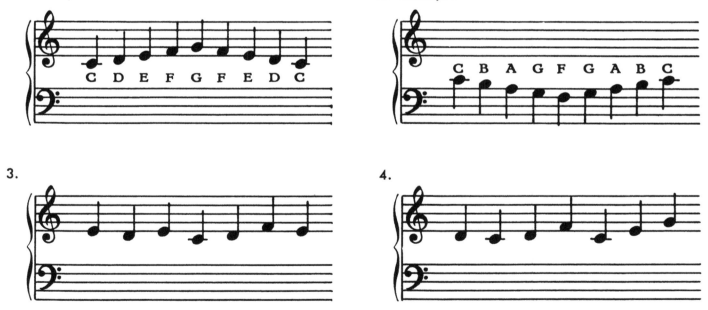

C D E F G F E D C

2. Example

C B A G F G A B C

3.

4.

How can you **see** the difference between D and E? E and F? E and G?

5.

6.

How can you **see** the difference between B and A? A and G? A and F?

NOTE VALUE REVIEW

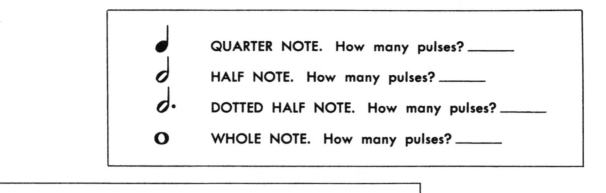

QUARTER NOTE. How many pulses? _____

HALF NOTE. How many pulses? _____

DOTTED HALF NOTE. How many pulses? _____

WHOLE NOTE. How many pulses? _____

A slur ⌒ groups notes together making a musical sentence which is called a PHRASE.

BAR LINES AND MEASURES

Bar lines divide music into small sections called MEASURES. A MEASURE is the distance from one bar line to the next.

MEASURES divide the pulses into groups of equal numbers.

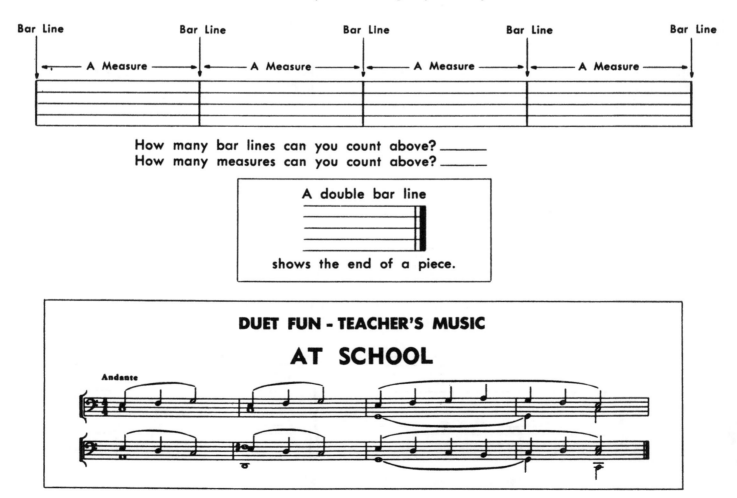

How many bar lines can you count above? _____
How many measures can you count above? _____

A double bar line

shows the end of a piece.

DUET FUN - TEACHER'S MUSIC

AT SCHOOL

Andante

TIME SIGNATURES

PRACTICE PLAN

1. Say and tap the words.
2. How many measures do you see? _____
3. How many pulses do you feel in each measure? _____
4. Do you see a number at the beginning of the piece which tells you how many pulses are in each measure?
5. What kind of note receives one pulse? _____
   Do you see this kind of note printed under the number? Circle it.

KEEP YOUR EYES ON THE NOTES — PLAY STRAIGHT THROUGH WITHOUT STOPPING

Write the names of the notes you will play in this piece.

AT SCHOOL

In walking time

Play and draw
R.H. Middle C and a step up.

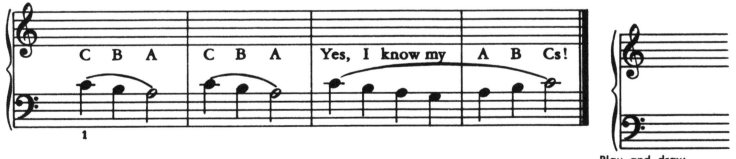

Play and draw
L.H. Middle C and a step down.

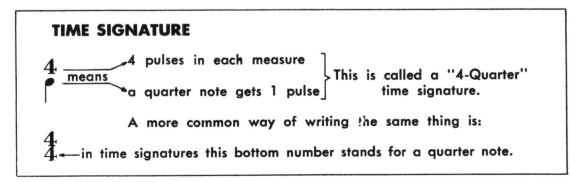

TIME SIGNATURE

4 means → 4 pulses in each measure
a quarter note gets 1 pulse } This is called a "4-Quarter" time signature.

A more common way of writing the same thing is:

4/4 — in time signatures this bottom number stands for a quarter note.

W. M. Co. 9585

PRACTICE PLAN

1. Say and tap the words.
2. How many measures do you see? _____
3. How many pulses do you feel in each measure? _____
4. Do you see a number at the beginning of the piece which tells you how many pulses are in each measure?
5. What kind of note receives one pulse? _____
   Circle the number that stands for this note in the time signature.

KEEP YOUR EYES ON THE NOTES — PLAY STRAIGHT THROUGH WITHOUT STOPPING

Write the names of the notes you will play in this piece.

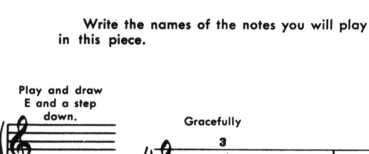

Play and draw E and a step down.

SKATING

Gracefully

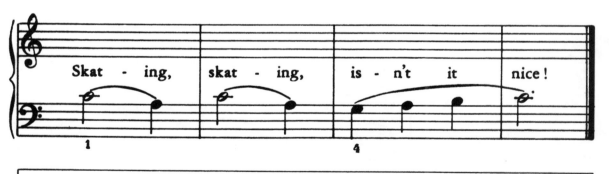

Skat - ing, skat - ing, o - ver the ice.

Skat - ing, skat - ing, is - n't it nice!

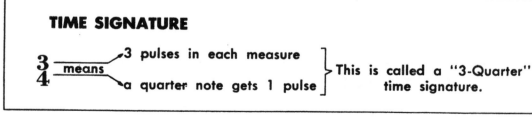

Play and draw A and a step up.

TIME SIGNATURE

$\frac{3}{4}$ means → 3 pulses in each measure / a quarter note gets 1 pulse ⎫ This is called a "3-Quarter" time signature.

DUET FUN - TEACHER'S MUSIC

PRACTICE PLAN

1. Say and tap the words.
2. How many measures do you see? _____
3. How many pulses do you feel in each measure? _____
4. Do you see a number at the beginning of the piece which tells you how many pulses are in each measure?
5. What kind of note receives one pulse? _____
   Circle the number that stands for this kind of note in the time signature.

KEEP YOUR EYES ON THE NOTES — PLAY STRAIGHT THROUGH WITHOUT STOPPING

Write the names of the notes you will play in this piece.

MONKEY, MONKEY

Play and draw
D and a step up.

In moderate time

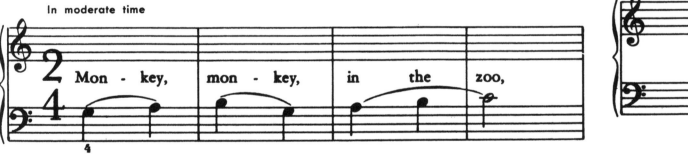

Mon - key, mon - key, in the zoo,

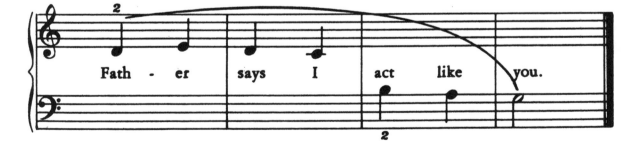

Fath - er says I act like you.

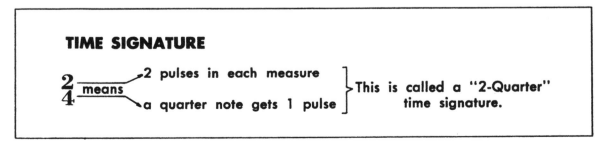

Play and draw
G and a skip up.

TIME SIGNATURE

$\frac{2}{4}$ means — 2 pulses in each measure
— a quarter note gets 1 pulse ⎬ This is called a "2-Quarter" time signature.

W. M. Co. 9585

PRACTICE PLAN

1. Say and tap the words.
2. How many measures do you see? _____
3. How many pulses do you feel in each measure? _____
4. Do you see a number at the beginning of the piece which tells you how many pulses are in each measure?
5. What kind of note receives one pulse? _____
   Circle the number that stands for this kind of note in the time signature.

KEEP YOUR EYES ON THE NOTES — PLAY STRAIGHT THROUGH WITHOUT STOPPING

Write the names of the notes you will play in this piece.

BICYCLE

Moving along

Bi - cy - cle, bi - cy - cle,   don't be late.   You know it's al-read - y   half past eight.

Turn 'round the cor-ner and   to   the right.   Then in a min-ute our   school's in sight.

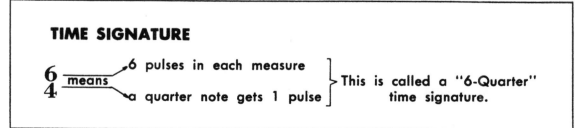

TIME SIGNATURE

$\frac{6}{4}$ means — 6 pulses in each measure — a quarter note gets 1 pulse } This is called a "6-Quarter" time signature.

W. M. Co. 9585

PRACTICE PLAN

1. What is the time signature of both pieces? _____
2. Say and tap the words.

MAGICIAN

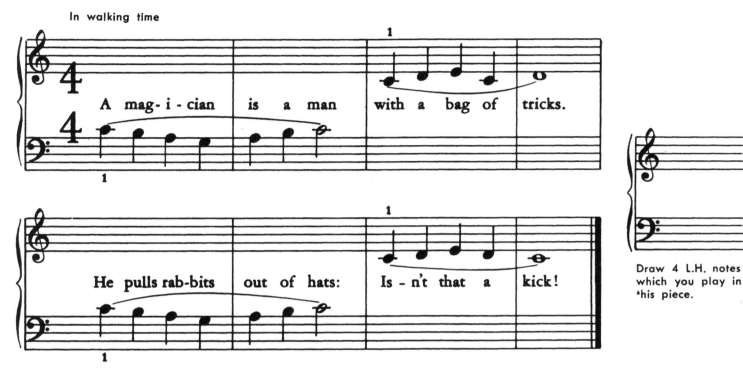

Draw 4 L.H. notes which you play in this piece.

SUMMER CAMP

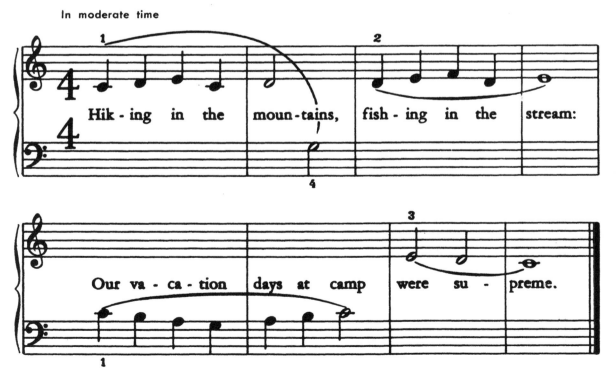

Draw 4 R.H. notes which you play in this piece.

W. M. Co. 9585

Unit 2
CHORDS

A chord is formed by playing three keys at the same time.
Chords make HARMONY in music.

Below are 4 keyboard pictures of chords.

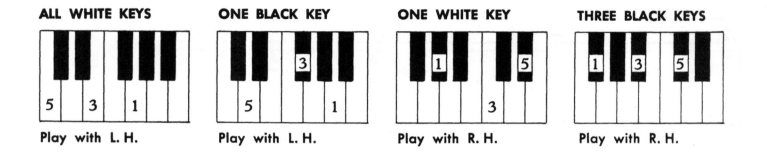

ALL WHITE KEYS — Play with L. H.
ONE BLACK KEY — Play with L. H.
ONE WHITE KEY — Play with R. H.
THREE BLACK KEYS — Play with R. H.

Play the chords above with the opposite hand. Reverse the bottom and top finger numbers.
(If the 2nd and 4th fingers are hard to control, lift them up with the other hand for a few practices.)

PRACTICE PLAN

1. Sing the words and play the "ALL WHITE KEYS" chord from the pictures above.
2. Play the chord while your teacher plays the melody on the piano.

ARE YOU SLEEPING
(Duet for Teacher and Pupil)

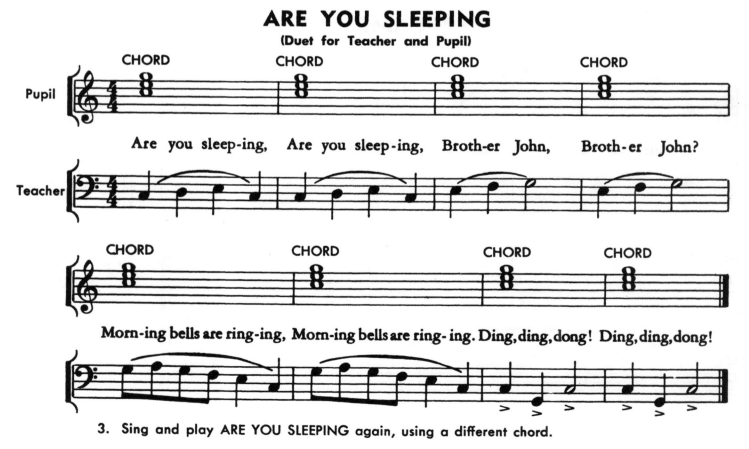

3. Sing and play ARE YOU SLEEPING again, using a different chord.

W. M. Co. 9585

PRACTICE PLAN

1. Sing and play the "ONE BLACK KEY" chord from the pictures on the preceding page.
2. Play the chord while your teacher plays the melody on the piano.

BUGLE CALL
(Duet for Teacher and Pupil)

Teacher

You can't stay in bed, you can't stay in bed. Get up with the morn-ing sun-rise. There's

Pupil

CHORD   CHORD   CHORD   CHORD

work to be done and wars to be won. Get up with the morn-ing sun.

CHORD   CHORD   CHORD   CHORD

PRACTICE PLAN   CHINESE MELODY

1. Play the "ALL BLACK KEYS" chord from the pictures on the preceding page while your teacher plays the melody.

Teacher

This is an an-cient Chi-nese mel - o - dy

Pupil

CHORD   CHORD   CHORD   CHORD

which has been sung through ma-ny cen-tur - ies.

CHORD   CHORD   CHORD   CHORD

W. M. Co. 9585

BLOCKED CHORDS - BROKEN CHORDS

When you play the notes of a chord all together, you are playing a BLOCKED CHORD.
When you play the notes of a chord one at a time, you are playing a BROKEN CHORD.

1. Play the C Major chord with your right hand.
   Name the notes you skipped: _____ and _____. Draw them.

2. Underline the correct answer:
   The C Major chord gets its name from (the bottom note; the middle note; the top note) of the chord.

Practice Plan

1. What is the time signature? _____
2. Say and tap the words.

Before you play, touch the keys. Then
KEEP YOUR EYES ON THE NOTES — PLAY STRAIGHT THROUGH WITHOUT STOPPING

CHORDS

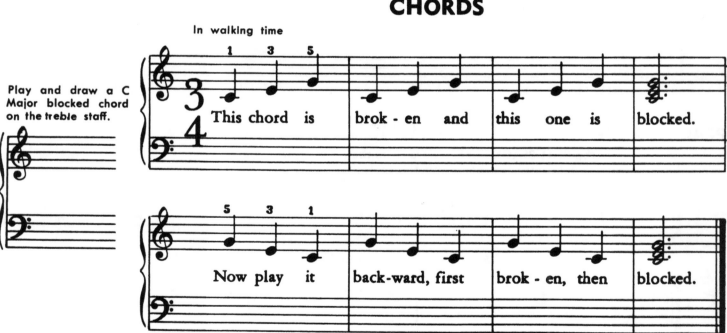

Play and draw a C Major blocked chord on the treble staff.

Learn to play this piece

1. With your L. H., starting with the 5th finger on the first C below Middle C.
2. With your R.H., using the chord with two black keys.
3. With your L. H., using the chord with one black key.

Play the C Major chord in as many places as you can on the keyboard.

C Major Chord on the BASS STAFF

1. Play this C Major chord with your L. H.
   Name the notes you skipped: _____ and _____.
   Draw these notes.

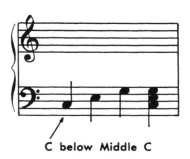

C below Middle C

BELLS

Play 1 octave higher

Slowly

Hear the bells ring - ing. What are they sing -

ing? Ding, dong, Ding, dong.

Play 1 octave lower

Play and draw a C Major blocked chord on the bass staff.

GEORGE AND ANDREW

In walking time

George and An-drew are my friends who have a swim-ming pool. (Splash!)

In the sum-mer when it's hot we jump in to get cool. (Splash!)

Draw the sign that means "Play 1 octave higher."

Draw the sign that means "Play 1 octave lower."

W. M. Co. 9585

FIRST CHORD PATTERN *(All White Keys)*

C MAJOR CHORD   F MAJOR CHORD   G MAJOR CHORD

1. Play these chords in as many places on the keyboard as you can.
2. Play them both blocked and broken, up and down the keyboard, until you know them from memory.

Every chord gets its name from the lowest tone.
This is called the ROOT TONE.

MINOR CHORDS

All Major Chords become Minor Chords when you move your 3rd finger to the **very next key** down the keyboard.

In the chords above, is this key black or white? _____

Play the chords of C Minor, F Minor and G Minor, both blocked and broken, up and down the keyboard, until you know them from memory.

BROKEN CHORD ARPEGGIOS

Sing the letter names.

C MAJOR   F MAJOR   G MAJOR   C MAJOR

C E G C E G   F A C F A C   G B D G B D   C E G C

CHORD SEQUENCES

Play the following chord sequences, first with R. H.; then with L. H.

    1. C Major — C Minor — C Major
    2. F Major — F Minor — F Major
    3. G Major — G Minor — G Major

Close your eyes: Can you hear if your teacher is playing a major or a minor chord?
Can you find on the piano the same chord your teacher played?

W. M. Co. 9585

Name the circled chords in each of the pieces below.

PUZZLE: Can you circle two more chords in INDEPENDENCE DAY?

INDEPENDENCE DAY

MERRY-GO-ROUND

Melody moves from one hand to the other.

PUZZLE: Can you circle four more chords in MERRY-GO-ROUND?

W. M. Co. 9585

1. Circle 3 notes in the first measure which form a chord you know.
   Name the chord: _____
2. Draw this chord on the staff in the margin.

THANKSGIVING DAY

In November there's a day set a-side for prayer

To give thanks for all things good, here and ev-'ry-where.

Name the circled chord below.
PUZZLE: Can you circle 3 more chords just like it?

DING DONG BELL

Ding-Dong Bell! Ding-Dong Bell! Pus-sy's fall-en in the well.

Ding-Dong Bell! Ding-Dong Bell! Call the Fire De-part-ment.

W. M. Co. 9585

Name the circled chords.

Can you circle other chords you know in this piece?

PUSSY CAT, PUSSY CAT

Gracefully

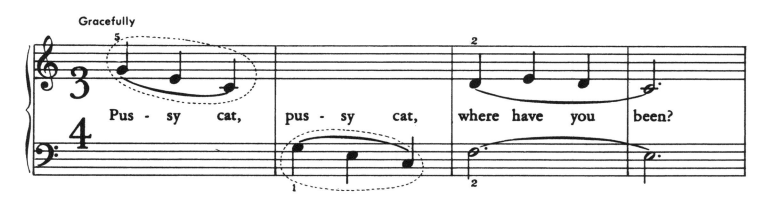

Pus - sy cat, pus - sy cat, where have you been?

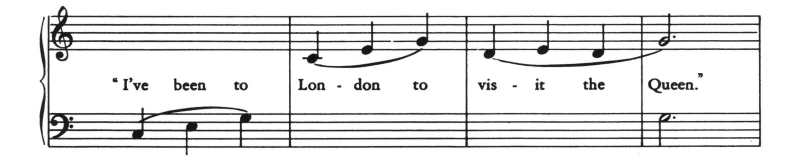

"I've been to Lon - don to vis - it the Queen."

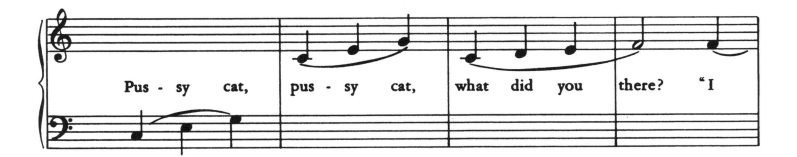

Pus - sy cat, pus - sy cat, what did you there? "I

fright - ened a lit - tle mouse un - der her chair."

W. M. Co. 9585

Unit 3

SHARPS, FLATS and NATURALS

♯ To make a key sharp (♯), play the very next key UP the keyboard.
Sharps are usually black keys, but there are 2 white-key sharps.

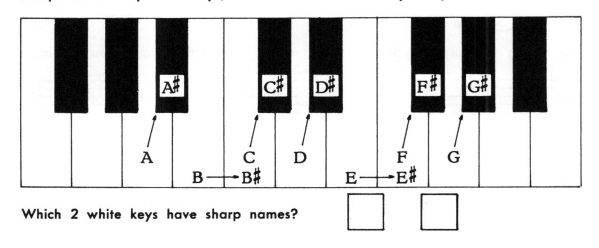

Which 2 white keys have sharp names?

♭ To make a key flat (♭), play the very next key DOWN the keyboard.
Flats are usually black keys, but there are 2 white-key flats.

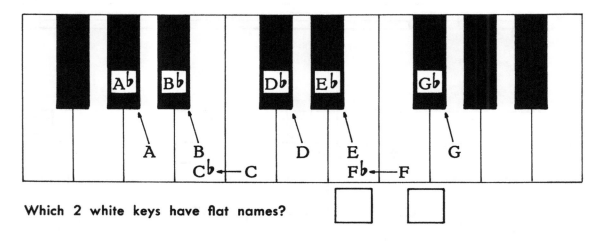

Which 2 white keys have flat names?

♮ A natural sign is used to cancel a ♯ or a ♭. Natural (♮) notes are
always white keys.

Color the following sharps and flats which are black keys.
Do not color the white-key sharps and flats.

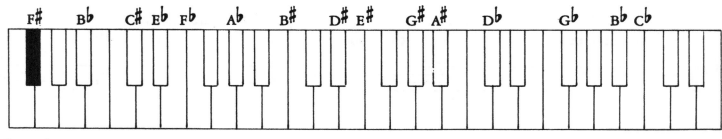

Example

W. M. Co. 9585

Write the names of the keys marked sharp (♯):

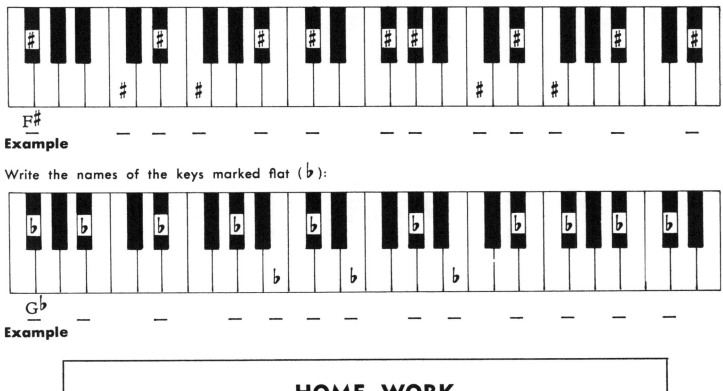

F♯
— — — — — — — — — —
Example

Write the names of the keys marked flat (♭):

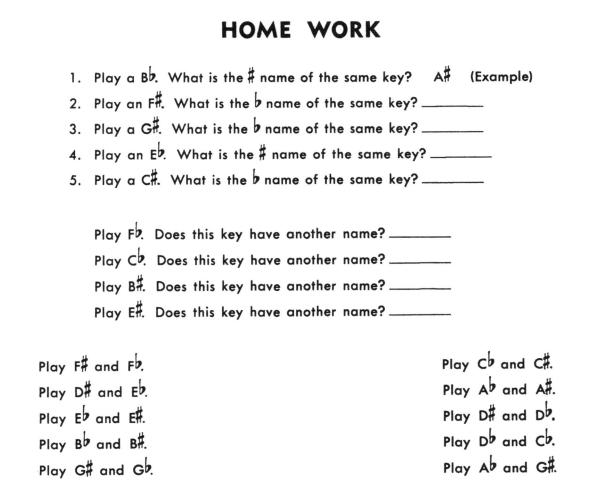

G♭
— — — — — — — — — —
Example

HOME WORK

1. Play a B♭. What is the ♯ name of the same key?   A♯   (Example)

2. Play an F♯. What is the ♭ name of the same key? _____

3. Play a G♯. What is the ♭ name of the same key? _____

4. Play an E♭. What is the ♯ name of the same key? _____

5. Play a C♯. What is the ♭ name of the same key? _____

Play F♭. Does this key have another name? _____

Play C♭. Does this key have another name? _____

Play B♯. Does this key have another name? _____

Play E♯. Does this key have another name? _____

Play F♯ and F♭.

Play D♯ and E♭.

Play E♭ and E♯.

Play B♭ and B♯.

Play G♯ and G♭.

Play C♭ and C♯.

Play A♭ and A♯.

Play D♯ and D♭.

Play D♭ and C♭.

Play A♭ and G♯.

BUMBLE BEE

HUMMING BIRD

TRICK OR TREAT

1. Name the circled chords.

*If a note which has already been a ♭ or ♯ occurs again in the same measure, you play it exactly as you played it before. It is not necessary to repeat the ♭ or ♯ sign. However, all ♭, ♯ and ♮ signs are cancelled by the bar line which ends the measure.

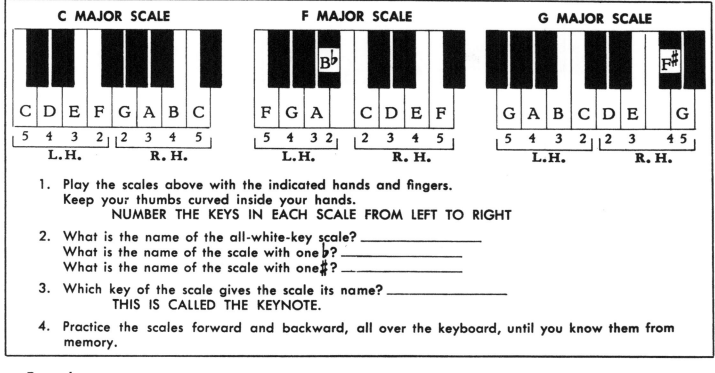

1. Play the scales above with the indicated hands and fingers.
   Keep your thumbs curved inside your hands.
   NUMBER THE KEYS IN EACH SCALE FROM LEFT TO RIGHT

2. What is the name of the all-white-key scale? _____
   What is the name of the scale with one ♭? _____
   What is the name of the scale with one ♯? _____

3. Which key of the scale gives the scale its name? _____
   THIS IS CALLED THE KEYNOTE.

4. Practice the scales forward and backward, all over the keyboard, until you know them from memory.

Example:

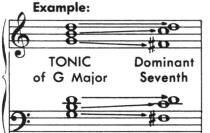

TONIC   Dominant
of G Major   Seventh

The major chords which you have learned (C Major, F Major, G Major) are formed by the 1st, 3rd and 5th tones of the scale with the same name. (Test this.)
    This is called the TONIC CHORD of its scale.

A TONIC CHORD can be changed to a DOMINANT SEVENTH CHORD by:

1. Repeating the 5th tone.
2. Moving from the 3rd tone **up** to the 4th tone.
3. Moving the lowest tone to the very next key **down** the keyboard.

STEP BY STEP

In walking time   (Using the scale tones and chords of the G MAJOR SCALE)

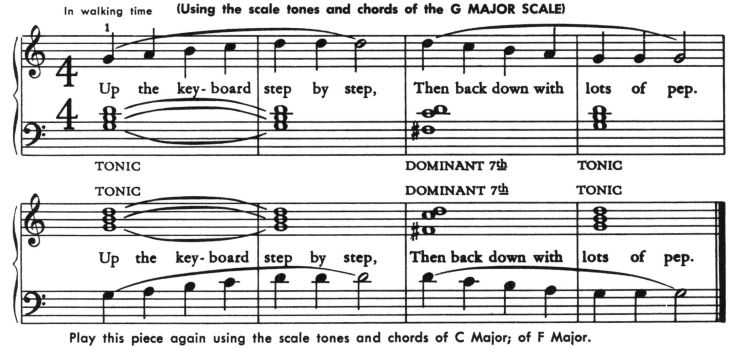

Play this piece again using the scale tones and chords of C Major; of F Major.

THIS IS CALLED TRANSPOSITION

Experiment: Can you transpose this tune to a minor sound? Change the tonic chord to minor, and let your ear help with the melody.

HALF TONES AND WHOLE TONES ON THE KEYBOARD

SOME HALF TONE PICTURES

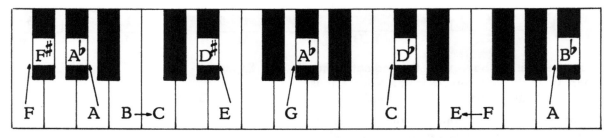

1. Following the direction of the arrows, play these HALF TONES.
2. Did you skip a key as you played each group of two keys? _____

SOME WHOLE TONE PICTURES

1. Following the direction of the arrows, play these WHOLE TONES.
2. Did you skip a key as you played each group of two keys? _____

EXPLAIN THE DIFFERENCE BETWEEN HALF TONES AND WHOLE TONES

All major scales are built with whole tones and half tones in an order that is always the same.

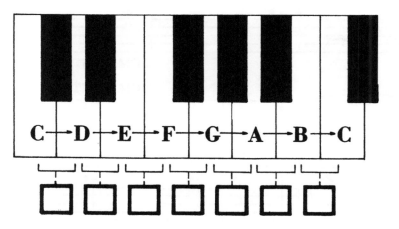

1. In the boxes write W for Whole tone and H for Half tone.
2. How many keys are in a major scale? Number them from left to right.
3. Between which numbers do the Half tones occur?

W. M. Co. 9585

SCALE DUETS

24

DYNAMICS SIGNS: *p* and *f*

p means PLAY SOFTLY (from the Italian word, "piano").
(Variants: *mp*, **mezzo piano**, means MODERATELY SOFTLY; *pp*, **pianissimo**, means VERY SOFTLY).
Circle any of these that you see in the piece below.

SLEEPY SONG

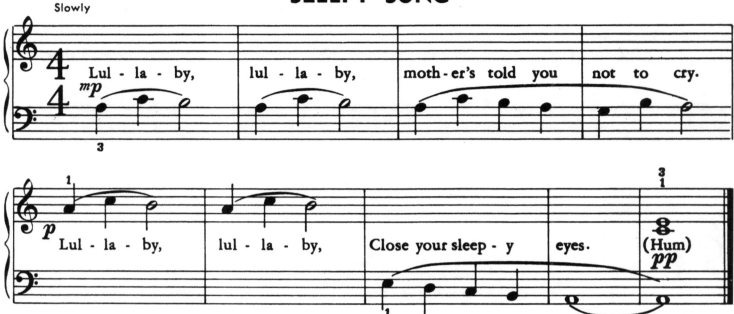

f means PLAY LOUDLY (from the Italian word, "forte").
(Variants: *mf*, **mezzo forte**, means MODERATELY LOUDLY; *ff*, **fortissimo**, means VERY LOUDLY).
Circle any of these that you see in the piece below.

THE BUGLER

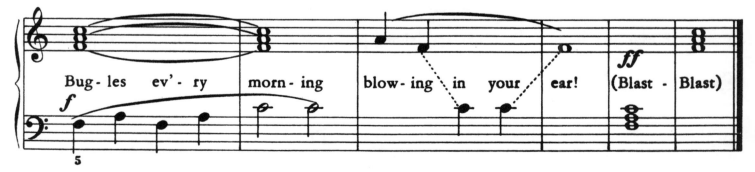

Name the circled chords.

Can you circle other chords in THE BUGLER?

W. M. Co. 9585

STACCATO TOUCH

A dot above or below a note (♪ ♩) shortens its sound. Release it quickly.
Circle all *p*s and *f*s you see on this page.

AT THE ZOO

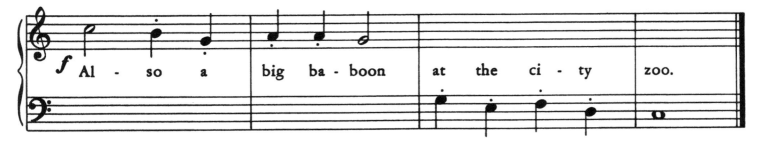

FOLLOW THE LEADER

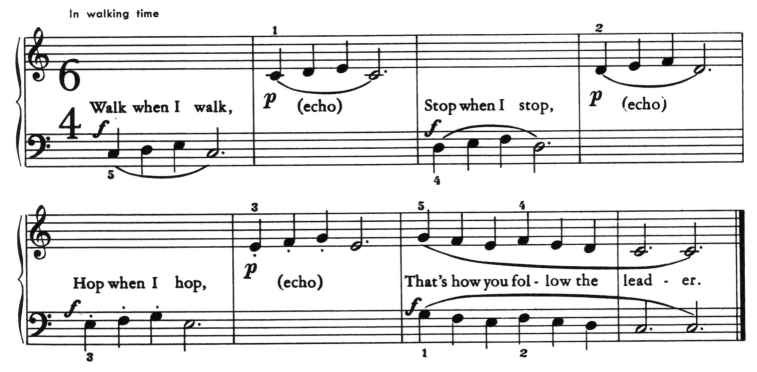

W. M. Co. 9585

Unit 4

HOW TO COUNT PULSES IN QUARTER TIME $\left(\frac{2}{4}-\frac{3}{4}-\frac{4}{4}-\frac{6}{4}\right)$

Most piano pieces do not have words. In order to play correct note values ALL MUSICIANS learn how to COUNT pulses.

The following chart shows three different ways to count in 4-Quarter time:

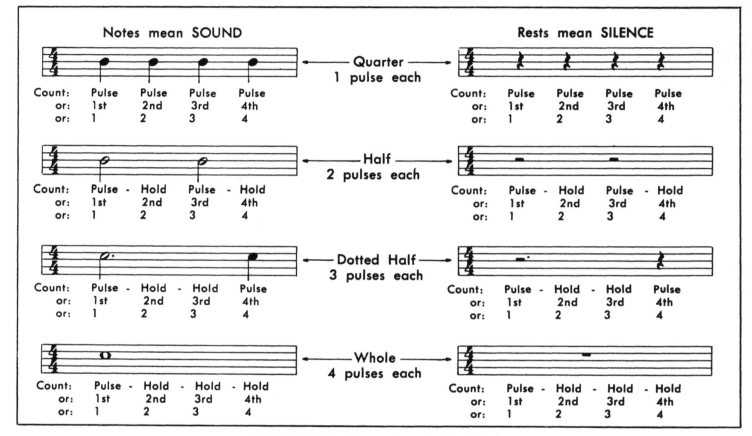

RHYTHM READINESS

Write the "Pulses" (P) and "Holds" (H.)
Then tap and count with the metronome set at 72 for one pulse.

Count and play the pulses in heavy type a little louder.

Play all pieces on this page slowly and firmly.

TWO-QUARTER TIME

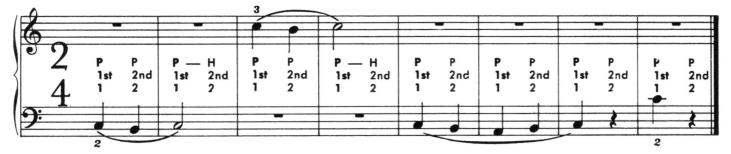

THREE-QUARTER TIME

FOUR-QUARTER TIME

SIX-QUARTER TIME

SPECIAL: A whole rest receives all the pulses of one measure.

W. M. Co. 9585

SECOND CHORD PATTERN

(White Key - Black Key - White Key)

1. Play these chords in as many places on the keyboard as you can.
2. Play them both blocked and broken, up and down the keyboard, until you know them from memory.

Every chord gets its name from (the lowest tone; the middle tone; the highest tone). Underline the answer.

This tone is called the _____ TONE.

MINOR CHORDS

A Major Chord can be changed to a Minor Chord by lowering the (lowest tone; the middle tone; the highest tone) a half tone. Underline the answer.

Play the chords of D Minor, E Minor and A Minor, both blocked and broken, up and down the keyboard until you know them from memory.

1. How many major chords do you know from memory? _____
2. How many minor chords do you know from memory? _____

BROKEN CHORD ARPEGGIOS

Sing the letter names.

CHORD SEQUENCES

Play the following chord sequences, first with R. H.; then with L. H.

1. D Major - D Minor - D Major
2. E Major - E Minor - E Major
3. A Major - A Minor - A Major

Close your eyes: Can you hear if your teacher is playing a major or a minor chord?
Can you find on the piano the same chord your teacher played?

W. M. Co. 9585

INTERVALS

The musical term for a STEP is "Interval of a 2nd;" for a SKIP, "Interval of a 3rd". It is important to be able to recognize other intervals as shown on the chart below, **BLOCKED** and **BROKEN**.

A GAY WALTZ

Waltz tempo (TEMPO means the time, or speed, at which you play a piece.)

Find an interval of a 3rd in this line.

Find an interval of a 2nd in this line.

Find an interval of a 3rd, a 4th, a 5th in this line.

On the chalk board or in your manuscript book write intervals of 4ths and 5ths, as your teacher directs.

Name the circled chords.

Can you circle other chords you know in this piece?

FROM NOW ON IN THIS BOOK, NAME ALL CIRCLED CHORDS AND CIRCLE ALL OTHER CHORDS YOU KNOW.

W. M. Co. 9585

REPEAT SIGN

1st ending :|| 2nd ending

The 2nd ending is played in place of the 1st ending after the repeat.

A RAINY DAY

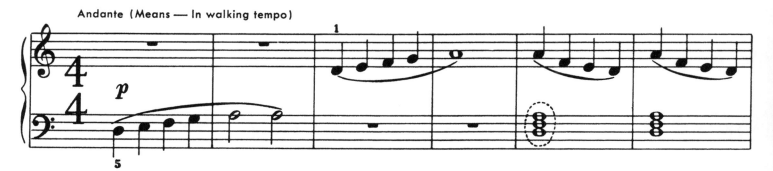

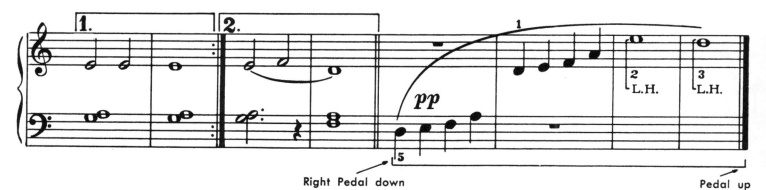

Right Pedal down   Pedal up

Circle and name any chords you recognize.

WINTER NIGHT

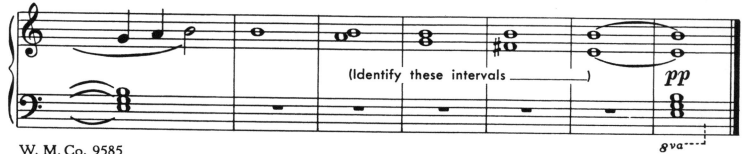

(Identify these intervals _____)

W. M. Co. 9585

THREE SCALE PICTURES

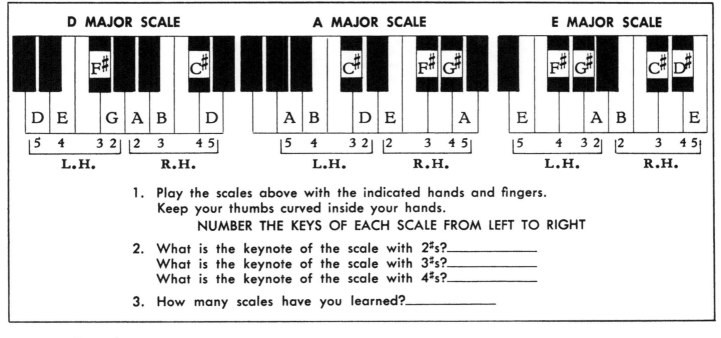

1. Play the scales above with the indicated hands and fingers.
   Keep your thumbs curved inside your hands.
   NUMBER THE KEYS OF EACH SCALE FROM LEFT TO RIGHT

2. What is the keynote of the scale with 2#s?_____
   What is the keynote of the scale with 3#s?_____
   What is the keynote of the scale with 4#s?_____

3. How many scales have you learned?_____

Example:

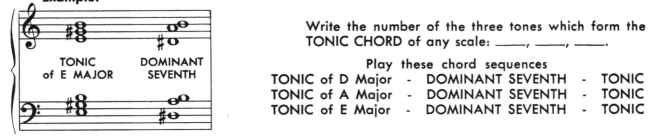

TONIC   DOMINANT
of E MAJOR   SEVENTH

Write the number of the three tones which form the
TONIC CHORD of any scale: _____, _____, _____.

Play these chord sequences
TONIC of D Major - DOMINANT SEVENTH - TONIC
TONIC of A Major - DOMINANT SEVENTH - TONIC
TONIC of E Major - DOMINANT SEVENTH - TONIC

STEP BY STEP
(Using the scale tones and chords of the E MAJOR SCALE)

Transpose this piece, using the scale tones and chords of D Major; A Major.

Transpose this piece to a minor sound.

W. M. Co. 9585

How many scales do you see in this piece? _____
Name them.

A SCALE PIECE

Moderato

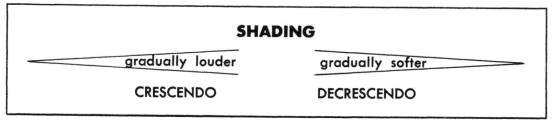

(Identify intervals)

SHADING		
gradually louder		gradually softer
CRESCENDO		DECRESCENDO

W. M. Co. 9585

Da Capo al Fine (D.C. al Fine) means "Repeat from the beginning and end with the measure where you see Fine".

DANCING SCHOOL

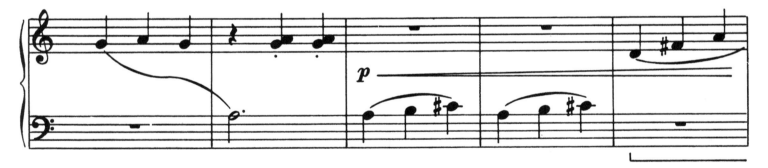

(Identify intervals in L. H. _ _ _ _ _ _ _ _ _ _ _ _ _ _ _ _ _ _

_)   D.C. al Fine

W. M. Co. 9585

EIGHTH NOTES

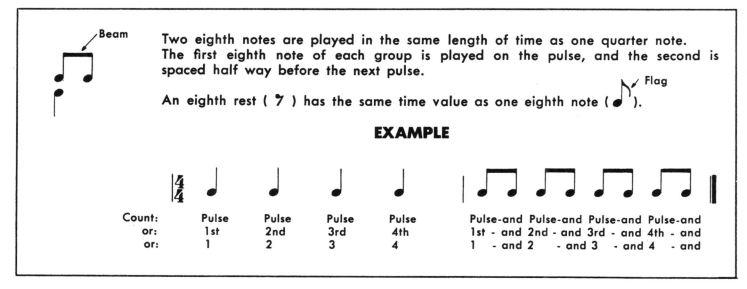

RHYTHM READINESS

Write the Pulses (P), the Holds (H) and the Ands (+).

Then tap and count with the metronome set at 72 for 1 pulse.

THE DOWN-BEAT - THE UP-BEAT

The first pulse of all measures is indicated by a down movement (DOWN-BEAT) of the conductor's baton, and the last pulse of all measures is indicated by an up movement (UP-BEAT) of the baton. Many pieces start on the UP-BEAT. When this is the case, this pulse added to the pulses of the last measure of the piece make one complete measure.

ACCENT TOUCH

>

This symbol above or below a note means that the note gets special emphasis.

SAILOR'S DANCE

Spiritoso (In spirited tempo — a little faster than Moderato)

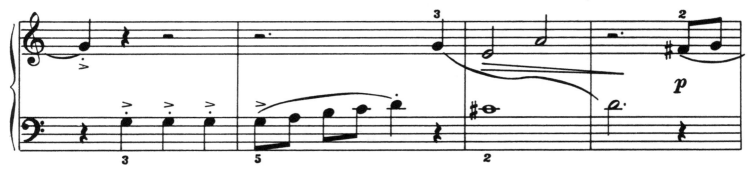

(Identify intervals in L. H.)

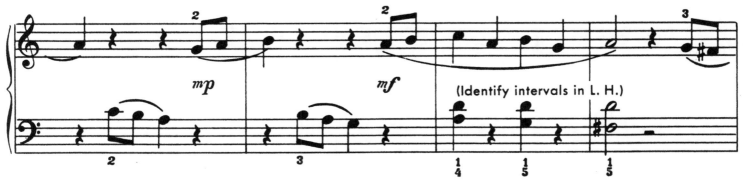

THIRD CHORD PATTERN
(BLACK KEY - WHITE KEY - BLACK KEY)

1. Play these chords in as many places as you can on the keyboard.
2. Play them both blocked and broken, up and down the keyboard, until you know them from memory.

Every chord gets its name from (the lowest tone; the middle tone; the highest tone). Underline the answer.

This tone is called the _____ TONE.

MINOR CHORDS

A Major Chord can be changed to a Minor Chord by lowering the (lowest tone; the middle tone; the highest tone) a half tone. Underline the answer.

Play the chords of D-Flat Minor, E-Flat Minor and A-Flat Minor, both blocked and broken, up and down the keyboard, until you know them from memory.

1. How many major chords do you know from memory? _____
2. How many minor chords do you know from memory? _____

BROKEN CHORD ARPEGGIOS

Sing the letter names.

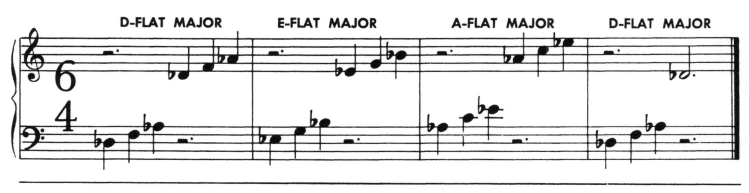

CHORD SEQUENCES

Play the following chord sequences, first with R. H.; then with L. H.

1. D-Flat Major - D-Flat Minor - D-Flat Major
2. E-Flat Major - E-Flat Minor - E-Flat Major
3. A-Flat Major - A-Flat Minor - A-Flat Major

Close your eyes: Can you hear if your teacher is playing a major or a minor chord?
Can you find on the piano the same chord your teacher played?

HORN PIECE

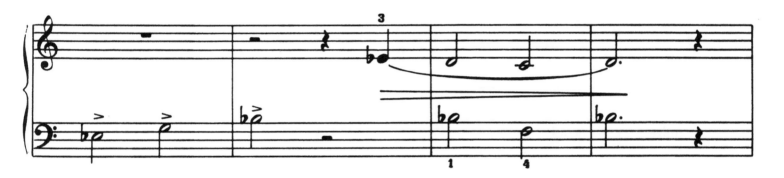

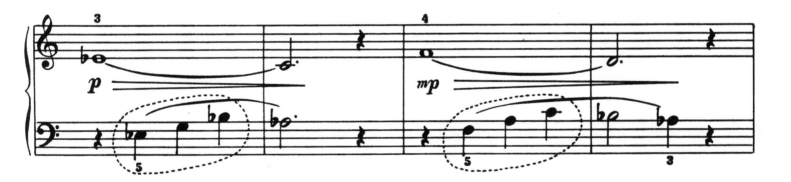

W. M. Co. 9585

38

This symbol above or below a note means that the note gets a slight emphasis.

A GHOST STORY

(Identify intervals in L. H. _ _ _ _ _ _ _ _ _ _ _ _ _ _)

*Coda

*A CODA is a special new musical theme added to the end of a piece.

W. M. Co. 9585

THREE SCALE PICTURES

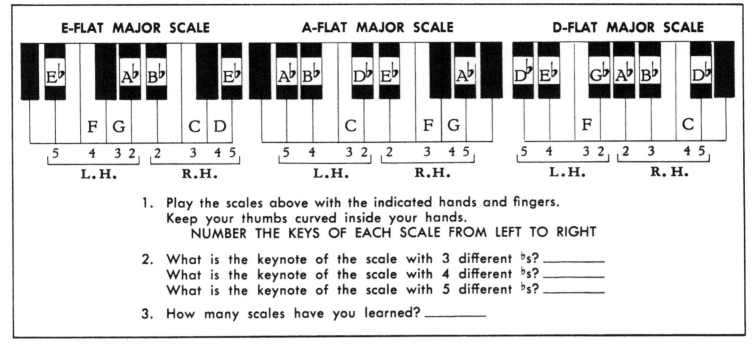

1. Play the scales above with the indicated hands and fingers.
   Keep your thumbs curved inside your hands.
   NUMBER THE KEYS OF EACH SCALE FROM LEFT TO RIGHT

2. What is the keynote of the scale with 3 different ♭s? _____
   What is the keynote of the scale with 4 different ♭s? _____
   What is the keynote of the scale with 5 different ♭s? _____

3. How many scales have you learned? _____

Example:

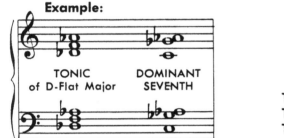

TONIC of D-Flat Major   DOMINANT SEVENTH

Write the numbers of the tones which form the TONIC
CHORD of any scale: ____, ____, ____.

Play these chord sequences
TONIC of E-Flat Major - DOMINANT SEVENTH - TONIC
TONIC of A-Flat Major - DOMINANT SEVENTH - TONIC
TONIC of D-Flat Major - DOMINANT SEVENTH - TONIC

STEP BY STEP

(Using the scale tones and chords of the D-Flat Major Scale)

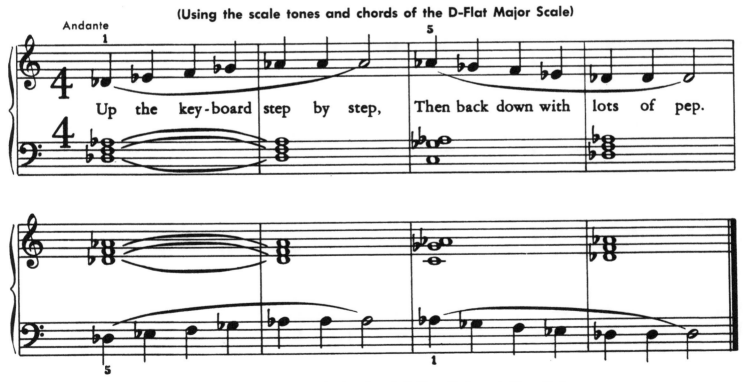

Transpose this piece, using the scale tones and chords of E-Flat Major; A-Flat Major.

Transpose this piece to a minor sound.

W. M. Co. 9585

Ritardando (rit.) means gradually slower.

a tempo means in time, again.

A Fermata (⌢) over a note or a rest means hold or pause.

BIRTHDAY PARTY

Waltz tempo

W. M. Co. 9585

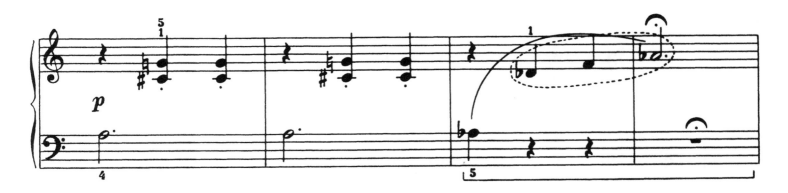

W. M. Co. 9585

Unit 6

ANOTHER WAY TO PRINT EIGHTH NOTES

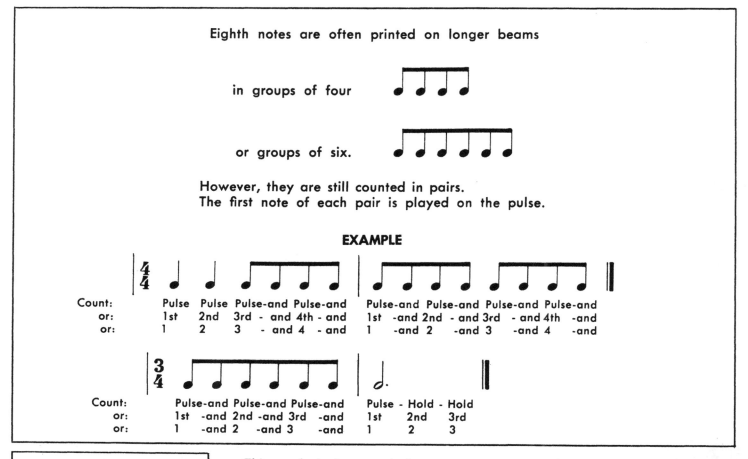

Eighth notes are often printed on longer beams

in groups of four

or groups of six.

However, they are still counted in pairs.
The first note of each pair is played on the pulse.

EXAMPLE

Count:	Pulse	Pulse	Pulse-and	Pulse-and	Pulse-and	Pulse-and	Pulse-and	Pulse-and
or:	1st	2nd	3rd - and	4th - and	1st -and	2nd - and	3rd - and	4th -and
or:	1	2	3 - and	4 - and	1 -and	2 -and	3 -and	4 -and

Count:	Pulse-and	Pulse-and	Pulse-and	Pulse - Hold - Hold
or:	1st -and	2nd -and	3rd -and	1st 2nd 3rd
or:	1 -and	2 -and	3 -and	1 2 3

PORTATO TOUCH

This symbol above or below a note means emphasize slightly and disconnect, producing a bell-like tone.

A GRACEFUL WALTZ

Grazioso (Gracefully)

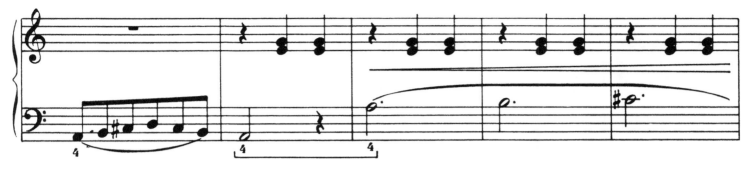

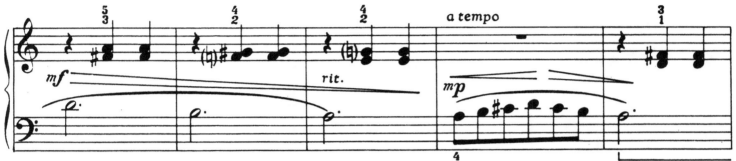

THE ODD CHORDS

1. Play these chords in as many places as you can on the keyboard.
2. Play them both blocked and broken, up and down the keyboard, until you know them from memory.
3. Do two of these chords sound exactly the same?

Every chord gets its name from (the lowest tone; the middle tone; the highest tone). Underline the answer.

This is called the _____ TONE.

MINOR CHORDS

A Major Chord can be changed to a Minor Chord by lowering the (lowest tone; the middle tone; the highest tone) a half tone. Underline the answer.

Play the chords of F-Sharp Minor, B Minor, B-Flat Minor and G-Flat Minor, both blocked and broken, up and down the keyboard, until you know them from memory.

1. How many major chords do you know from memory? _____
2. How many minor chords do you know from memory? _____

CHORD SEQUENCES

Play the following chord sequences, first with R. H.; then with L. H.

1. F-Sharp Major - F-Sharp Minor - F-Sharp Major
2. G-Flat Major - G-Flat Minor - G-Flat Major
3. B Major - B Minor - B Major
4. B-Flat Major - B-Flat Minor - B-Flat Major

Close your eyes: Can you hear if your teacher is playing a major or a minor chord?
Can you find on the piano the same chord your teacher played?

W. M. Co. 9585

MARCH OF THE SCOUTS

Brisk march tempo

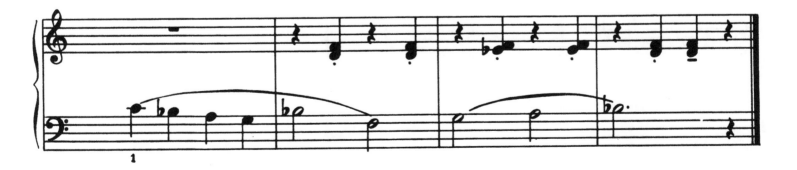

W. M. Co. 9585

LEGATO PEDAL

Pedal up and down quickly immediately after the note above

DRIFTING ALONG

Adagio (Very slowly)

THREE SCALE PICTURES

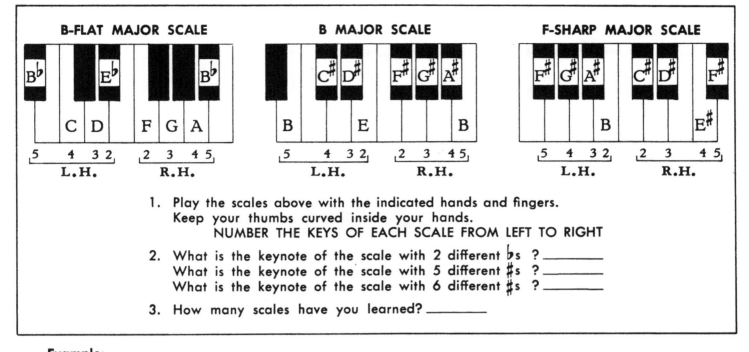

1. Play the scales above with the indicated hands and fingers.
   Keep your thumbs curved inside your hands.
   NUMBER THE KEYS OF EACH SCALE FROM LEFT TO RIGHT

2. What is the keynote of the scale with 2 different ♭s ? _____
   What is the keynote of the scale with 5 different ♯s ? _____
   What is the keynote of the scale with 6 different ♯s ? _____

3. How many scales have you learned? _____

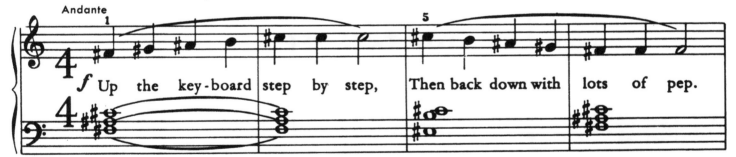

Example:

TONIC
of F-Sharp Major

DOMINANT
SEVENTH

Write the numbers of the tones which form the TONIC
CHORD of any scale: _____, _____, _____.

Play these chord sequences.
TONIC of B-Flat Major   - DOMINANT SEVENTH - TONIC
TONIC of B Major   - DOMINANT SEVENTH - TONIC
TONIC of F-Sharp Major - DOMINANT SEVENTH - TONIC

STEP BY STEP
(Using the scale tones and chords of the F-Sharp Major Scale)

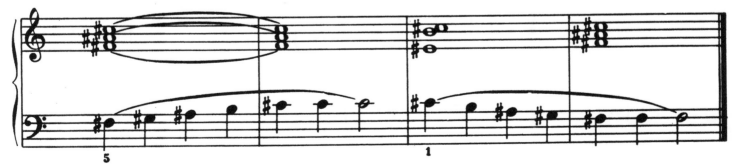

Andante

f Up the key-board step by step, Then back down with lots of pep.

Transpose this piece, using the scale tones and chords of B Major; B-Flat Major.
Transpose this piece to a minor sound.

W. M. Co. 9585

48

CHORD REVIEW IN HALF-TONE SEQUENCE

1. Practice each hand separately.
2. Practice hands together, one octave apart.

A capital letter means "Major"; a small letter means "minor".

TOY TRUMPET

W. M. Co. 9585